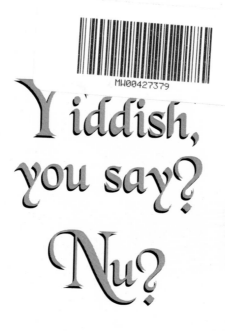

Yiddish, you say? Nu?

a Yiddish wordbook

from Kvetch *to* Kvell,
Klutz *to* Cockamamie,
Schmooze *to* Shlemiel

Sasha Newborn, editor

MUDBORN PRESS   2014   SΔNTΔ BΔRBΔRΔ

LITERARY FICTION

Family Secret, Last American Housewife, Period Pieces, Eleanore Hill
Aurora Leigh, E.B. Browning   Hadji Murad, Tolstoy   The Basement,
Newborn The First Detective. Poe   Matilda, Mary Shelley

SPECULATIVE FICTION

Frankenstein, Mary Shelley   The Martian Testament, Sasha Newborn

HISTORY

Mitos y Leyendas/Myths and Legends of Mexico. Bilingual
Beechers Through the 19th Century   Uncle Tom's Cabin, H. B. Stowe

SCHOOLING

Don't Panic: Procrastinator's Guide to Writing an Effective Term Paper
First Person Intense   Italian for Opera Lovers
French for Food Lovers Doctorese for the imPatient

SPIRITUAL

Ghazals of Ghalib   Gandhi on the *Bhagavad Gita*
Gospel According to Tolstoy Everlasting Gospel, William Blake

LOVE

Dante & His Circle. Love sonnets   Vita Nuova   Sappho

STAGING SHAKESPEARE

DIRECTOR'S PLAYBOOK SERIES: Hamlet   Merchant of Venice
Twelfth Night   Taming of the Shrew Midsummer Night's Dream Romeo
and Lydiat As You Like It Richard III Henry V Much Ado About Nothing
Macbeth Othello Julius Caesar King Lear Antony and Cleopatra

7 Plays with Transgender Characters   Falstaff: 4 Plays Venus and Adonis

TEACHERS ONLY

(*Q & A, glossaries, critical comments*)
Areopagitica, John Milton   Apology of Socrates, & Crito, Plato Leaves
of Grass, Walt Whitman   Sappho, The Poems

Foreword

In my short (five years) stay in New York City, I hadn't really thought about my home as the second most populous city of Jewry in the world. Although I never learned to read Yiddish or even thought about it much, it was all around me. Those two million Jews in the city helped mold the character of the city that I came to love.

This little book is an homage to this unique part of American culture, a piece of the melting pot that never quite melts away. As I look more closely at the extensive vocabulary, based in the Eastern European pan-national language called Yiddish, I recognize the deep humanity, involvement, and willingness to speak doubt, disgust, sexuality, as well as strength of character, honesty, and, yes, joy.

A number of Yiddish words have come into the sponge-language of American English, because no existing word quite fitted: cockamamie, shtick, bupkis, dreck, feh, and a great many pithy descriptions of personality types. Yiddish is also justly famous for its richness in insults, backhanded compliments, and sexual—well, you can't really call it innuendo.

If you find yourself in New York City, you may become a "New Yawker"; you'll need some of this lingo to keep up with conversations. Often you can glean the meaning of a word by the way it is said, as in, "Don't listen to him, he's meshugener."

Sasha Newborn
January 2014

Pronunciation

The Yiddish words in this dictionary are, as much as is possible, put into the roman alphabet of English. Yiddish was spoken over a large area of Europe and Russia, which gave rise to regional variations in pronunciation; consequently, some words are shown here with alternative spellings.

    The Yiddish alphabet contains a few letters of interest, that may clarify spelling and pronunciation. For example, ay, ey, oy, and y are single letters. So are k, k(q), and kh. The fricatives ts, tsh, tch, dzh, zh, dz, z, sh are all separate letters, though to the ear the sounds may seem almost indistinguishable. Some roman letters are not used at all: J, Q, X —while W and C are rarely used. "Alphabetical order" has been modified here to include some Yiddish letters, which may help to make some of these distinctions obvious.

    Single words are mixed with common sayings or expressions, here signified by quote marks; Yiddish is rich in aphorisms.

THE VOWELS

a as in father
ai as in Aye, aye, Sir.   BUT NOT as in rain
ay as in Aye, aye, Sir.
e as in let
eh (final) as in let
ey as in Hey, watch it!   BUT NOT as in key
i as in pizza   BUT NOT as in bit
o as in rope   BUT NOT as in of or soft
u (in middle) as in put   BUT NOT as in uh-huh or cute
u (word end) as in tune
y as in yes or try

THE CONSONANTS

Consonants are sounded forward in the mouth. Double con-sonants are given nearly double the amount of time (not-te).

NOT A PROBLEM, NO DIFFERENCE

b sounds as baby

d as in did

f as in food

m as in mama

l as in lily

s as in sister

z as in zebra

n as in nine

p as in papa

t as in tight

v as in verve

r as in rare

t as in teeter

SLIGHT DIFFERENCE

g is always hard, as in go

h (not in consonant cluster) as in hah

w (occurs rarely) is pronounced as v

BIG DIFFERENCE

c by itself sounds like k as in kick

tch sounds like ch as in church

tsh sounds more sibilant, as ch as cheek

dzh sounds like j as in judge

zh (voiced sh) as in mirage or azure

dz as in suds

kh sounds like a breathy k, or clearing the throat

tz sounds like ts as in hats

kn: both letters are pronounced, as in knish (k-nish)

A

"A bi gezunt": as long as you've got your health (nothing else matters)

"A breyre hob ikh": I have no choice

"A brokh!": Damn it!

"A brokh tzu dir!": A curse on you!

"A brokh tsu dayn lebn": May your life be a ruin

"A deigeh hob ikh": I should worry

"A foiler tut in tsveyen": A lazy person has to do the same job twice

"Afn gonif brennt das hittel": a thief's hat burns; he has a bad conscience

"A gesheft hob nikht": I don't care

"A glick hot dikh getrofen!": So what? You were lucky!

"Ahf mir gezogt!": If only they'd say that about me!

Ahf tsores: in trouble

Ahf zu lokhis: out of spite

Ahntoisht: disappointed

Ahzes ponim: impudent fellow

"A klog tzu meineh sonim!": A curse to my enemies!

"A khalerye": A plague on you; cholera to you

"A khazer bleibt a khazer": A pig is always a pig

"A khorbn": Oh, crap!

Akhrahyes: responsibility

"A klog is mir": Woe is me

"A leben ahf dir!": Live! Be well!

alef-baiz: the alphabet; the abc's

Aleikhem shalom: formal reply to the formal greeting Shalom aleikhem

"Alevei!": May this happen to me!

Aliyah: journey to Israel; reading the Torah aloud

Alrightnik/Alrightnikeh: successful man/woman

Alte kaker: an "old fart," complaining old man

Alteh makhashaifeh: old witch

Alteh moid: spinster, old maid

Alter bokher: bachelor

Alter bok: old goat

alter bakahnter: old acquaintance

alter trombenick: old bum

Amain: amen

"A mentsh trakht und Gott lakht": You plan and God laughs

A metsieh far a ganef: It's really cheap (a bargain for a thief)

Am-ha'aretz: ordinary or ignorant person

"A nahr bleibt a nahr": A fool is always a fool

"A nekhtiker tog!": Forget about it!

Apikoros: skeptic; atheist

Arbit: work

Arein: Come in!

Aroisgevorfen: wasted opportunity

"Aroisgevorfene gelt": a waste of money

Arumgeflickt!: milked!

Arumloifer: street person

Ashkenazi: Jew whose family came from middle or eastern Europe

"A shvarts yor": A miserable year (to you)

"A shandeh un a kharpeh": A shame and a disgrace

A shittern mogn: diarrhea

A shtyfer mogn: constipated

"A sof!": Let's end it !

A tukhes un a halb: a very large backside

Averah: sin

Avodah: worship; service.

"A volf farlirt zayne hor, ober nit zayn natur": A wolf loses his hair but not his nature.

"Az a yor ahf mir": I should have such luck

"Az mir vill shlugen a hunt, gifintmin a shtecken": To beat a dog, one finds a stick

"Az okh un vai!": Tough luck!

Azoy?: Really?

"Azoy gait es!": That's how it goes!

"Azoy gikh?": So soon?

"Azoy vert dos kikhel tzekrokhen!": That's how the cookie crumbles!

8

Ay

Aidel: finicky

Aidel gepotchket: cultured

Aidim: son-in-law

Ainikleh: grandchild

"Ain klaynigkeit": Ya, sure!

Aitzeh: advice

Aiver butelt: absent-minded

Ay-yay-yay: happy or ironic exclamation

B

Babka: coffee cake pastry

Badkhen: jester; emcee at a wedding

Baigel: hard bread roll in donut shape, not sweet

Bagroben: to bury

Baitsim: testicles

Balabusta: house mistress of importance; a bossy woman

Balebatim: persons of high standing

Balbatish: respectable, well mannered

Balebatisheh yiden: Jews of good reputation

Baleboss: man of the house

Balegoola: sloppy person of low standing

Balmalokha: an expert; self-proclaimed expert

Balnes: miracle-worker

Bal Toyreh: scholar

Balt: sure

Bandit: outlaw, pain-in-the-neck

Bareden yenem: to gossip

Baren: fornicate, annoy

Barimer: braggart, show-off

Bar mitzvah: a celebration of coming of age of a 13-year-old boy

Baruch Habah: welcome (spoken to men)

Bat mitzvah: celebrating the coming of age of a 12-year-old girl

Bashert: fated, destined

Bas-yekhide: A female only child

Batampte: tasty , delicious

Batlan: someone without a regular job

Bekher: wine glass

Behaimeh: animal, cow; dull-witted human

Bei Mir Bist du Shayn: To me you're beautiful (popular song title)

Benken: to long for

Benkshaft: nostalgia

Bentsh: to bless, recite a blessing

Bentshen lekht: prayer spoken over Sabbath eve or Holy Day candles

Ben-yokhid: a male only child

Beryeh: efficient housewife; woman with excellent homemaking skills

Bes din, Bet din: rabbinical court

Bes medresh: synagogue

Bialy: large chewy round yeast roll, sprinkled with chopped onion

Bikur kholem: visiting the sick

Billik: inexpensive

binah: wisdom

bisel: little bit

biseleh: very little bit

"Bist meshugeh?": Are you crazy?

Biteh: please

Blekh: belch

Blintz: pancake filled with cream cheese

Blondzhen: To wander, be lost

B'nai B'rith: sons of the covenant

B'nai Noakh: Sons of Noah; non-Jews who live by the Torah

Borderkeh: A female boarder

Bobbemyseh: old wives' tales, nonsense.

Bobeh, bubbeh: grandmother

Bokh: a punch

Bohmer: male bum

Bohmerkeh: female bum

Boreke borsht: fancy beet borsht

Borekes: pastries with cheese inside

Borsht: beet soup

Borsht Belt: Hotels in the Catskill Mountains for Jewish visitors; standup comics and singers work out their material at these hotels

Borviss: barefoot

Borvisser fiss: going barefoot

Botvenye borsht: borsht made from beet leaves for the poor

Boytchik: young boy

Boykh: stomach, abdomen

Boykhvehtig: stomachache

Brakha: a blessing

Breire: choice

Bris: circumcision

Bristen: breasts

Brokheh: blessing, prayer

Broitgeber: head of family

Bronfen: whiskey

Broygis: not on speaking terms

Brukha Habaha: welcome (spoken to women)

B'Shalom: in peace

B'Shira: in song

B'suleh: virgin

Bubbeh: grandmother

Bubbe maisse: grandmother's tale

Bubbee: friend, pal

Bubeleh: endearing term for anyone regardless of age

Buhheh-myseh: made-up story.

Bulvan: heavyset; boorish, rude person

Bupkis: nothing; worthless; absurd

Butchke: chat, gossip

C

Cockamamie: ridiculous, crazy

Cohen: Hebrew priest

> *See also* "K" for hard-k as in "kick"
> "Kh" for soft-k as if clearing the throat
> "Tch" for hard-ch as in "chess"

D

"Danken Got!": Thank G-d!

"Darf min gehn in kolledzh?": For this I went to college?

Daven: pray

Dayan (pl. dayanim): rabbinical judge

"Deigeh nisht!": Don't worry!

"Der menskhh trakht un Gott lahkht": Man plans and God laughs

"Der tate oysn oyg": Just like his father

Derekh erets: respect

Derlebn: To live to see; may I live that long!

"Dershtikt zolstu veren!": You should choke on it!

Diaspora: The worldwide dispersion of the Jews

"Dine Essen teg": eating days (for Yeshiva students fed on a rotating basis at various houses)

Dingen: bargain, hire, engage, lease, rent

"Dis fayntin shneg": It's starting to snow

"Dis fayntin zoraiganin": It's starting to rain

"Dos gefelt mir": This pleases me

"Dos hartz hot mir gezogt": My heart told me. I knew it.

"Dos iz alts": That's all

"Dos zelbeh": The same

Dover: Pray.

"Drai mir nit kain kop!": Don't twist my head. Don't bother me!

"Drai zikh!": Keep moving!

Draikop: scatterbrain

draydl: four-sided top played during Khanukah

Drek: manure or excrement; poor quality; unwarranted flattery; ugly

"Drek auf dem teller": dung on a plate; worthless; mean-spirited

Drek mit Leber: not worth anything whatsoever

Dreykop: confused person

Drukhus: the boonies; outskirts

"Du fangst shoyn on?": Are you starting up again?

"Du kannst nikht auf meinem rucken pishen unt mir sagen class es regen ist": You can't pee on my back while telling me that it's rain!

Dumkop: dummy

Durkhfall: flop; failure

Dybbuk: an evil spirit that controls a living person until exorcised

E

Ekh: Ick, Oof (a groan)

Ekh mir: not for me (You call that a _____?)

Efsher: maybe, could be

Ek velt: end of the world; nowhere

Emmes: truth

Emmisse meisse: a true tale

Emitzer: someone

Emunah: faith

Enshultig meir: "Pardon me!" (serious or ironic)

Entoisht: disappointed

Eppes: something; also, "Isn't that something!"

"Eppes a meshuga!": Truly a crazy guy!

"Er bolbet narishkeiten": He talks nonsense

"Er drayt sikh arum vie a fortz in russell": He wanders like a fart in a barrel; aimless, pointless

Eretz Yisrael: the land of Israel (not simply the State of Israel)

Erev Shabbat: the eve of a Sabbath

"Er est vi nokh a krenk": He eats like a sick person recovering

"Er frest vi a ferd": He eats like a horse

"Er hot a makeh": He has a boil (he's got nothing at all)

"Er hot nit zorg": He has nothing to worry about

"Er iz a niderrekhtiker kerl!": He's a no-good bum

"Er iz shoyn du, der nudnik!": Here he comes, the nuisance!

"Er makht a tel fun dem": He ruins it

"Er makht zack nisht visindikht": He acts as if he's not doing anything wrong.

"Er toig nit": He's no good, worthless

"Er varved zakh": He throws himself; he's getting worked up or pissed-off

"Er zitst oyf shpilkes": He's sitting on needles; restless

"Er zol vaksen vi a tsibeleh, mit dem kop in drerd!": He should grow like an onion, with his head in the ground!

"Es brent mir ahfen hartz": I have heartburn!

"Es gait nit!": This isn't working! It isn't running right!

"Es gefelt mir": I like it

"Es hot zikh oysgelohzen a boydem!": Nothing up there but a small attic; it was all for nothing

"Es iz a shandeh far di kinder!": It's a shame for the children!

"Es iz tsu shpet": It's too late

"Es ken gemolt zein": It is conceivable; it could happen

"Es makht mir nit oys": It doesn't matter to me

"Es iz nit dayn gesheft": It's none of your business

"Es mayn kind!": Eat my child!

"Es past nit": It is not becoming. It is not fitting

Ess: Eat

"Ess, benkh, sei a mensh": Eat, pray, man up!

"Ess gezunterhait": Eat in good health

Essen: To eat

Essen mitik: Eating midday or having dinner

"Es tut mir a groisseh hanoeh!": It gives me great pleasure! (serious, or ironic)

"Es tut mir bahng": I'm sorry.

"Es tut mir vai": It hurts me

"Es vert mir finster in di oygen": It's getting dark in my eyes (on hearing distressing news)

"Es vet gornit helfen!": Nothing will help!

"Es vet helfen vi a toiten bahnkes!": It won't help at all!

"Ess vie ein foygl sheise vie ein feirt!": Eat like a bird, shit like a horse!

Ey

Ei! Ei!: *See* Ay-yay-yay

Eingeshpahrt: stubborn

Eingetunken: dunked

Einhoreh: evil eye

Eizel: Fool, dope

Eytse: advice

F

Fakhadik: extremely confused

Famisched: confused

Fantazyor: person who builds castles in the air

Farbisene: bitter

Farbissener: embittered; sourpuss

Farblondzhet: lost, bewildered, confused

Farbludzhet: bending your ear

Farbrekher: crook, conman

Fardeiget: distressed, worried, full of care, anxiety

"Fardinen a mitzveh": Earn a blessing

Fardrayt: dizzy, confused.

"Fardrai zikh dem kop!": Go drive yourself crazy!

Fardross: resentment, disappointment, sorrow

Farfel: tiny noodles

Farfolen: lost

Farfoylt: mildewed, rotten, decayed

Farfroyren: frozen

Fargenign: delight

Fargessen: forgot

Farkatke: lousy, ridiculous, shitty

Farklempt, ferklempt. *See* **Verklempt**

Farklempt fis: clumsy on one's feet

Far knaft: engaged

Farkakt: screwed up, fucked up

Farkrimpt: scowling, annoyed

Farkrimpter ponim: scowling, twisted face

Farkrumte: crooked or twisted; perhaps twisted logic

"Farmakh dos moyl!": Shut your mouth! Quiet!

Farmatert: tired

Farmisht: befuddled, mixed up

Farmutshet: worn out, exhausted

Farpitz: all dressed up.

Farprishte punim: pimple-faced

Farschimmelt: moldy, rotten; senile

Farshikert: very drunk

Farshlepteh krenk: longterm sickness; fruitless, pointless activity

Farshmeyeter: high-energy person; always on the go

Farshnickert: drunk

Farshnoshket: drunk as a skunk

Farshtaist?: You understand?

Farshtinkener/fershtinkener: revolting, smelly; rotten person, a louse

Farshtopt: stuffed

Farshtunken: stinks, rotten

Farshvindn: disappeared

Farshvitst: sweaty

Fartik: finished, ready

Fartshadikt: confused, befuddled, gassed

Fartummelt: befuddled, confused

Faygeleh: homosexual; little bird

Feh!: Ugh! Fooey! It stinks! (as if spitting)

Feinkokhen: omelet, scrambled eggs

Feinshmeker: hifalutin

Fendel: pan

Ferd: horse; a fool

Fershlugginer: mixed-up, shaken; of dubious value; messed up, no good.

Fet: fat, obese

Fetter: uncle (also *onkel*)

Finster un glitshik: miserable

Fisfinger: toes

Fisslakh: chicken or duck feet, often in ptsha

Flayshedik: kosher meat dishes.

Fleischig: meaty

Fliegel: fowl's wing

Fokha: fan

Foigel: smart guy

Foiler: lazy man

Foilishtik: foolishness

"Folg mikh!": Obey me!

"Folg mikh a gang!": So far, why bother? It's hardly worth the effort!

Fonfen: nasal speaking

"For gezunterhait!": Travel in good health!

Forshpeiz: appetizer

Fortz: fart

Fortz n' zovver: foul-smelling fart

Frageh: question

Frailekh: happy

Frask: slap

Frassk in pisk: slap in the face

Freilikhen Yomtov: Have a pleasant festival

Freint: friend

Fremder: stranger

Fress: eat like an animal; eating noisily and in great quantity; pig out

Fresser: pig, eating like a pig

Freylokh: happy, joyful

Froy: woman, Mrs.

Frum, fromm: observant; orthodox

Frummer: religious person

Fuftsike: $50 bill

Funfeh: speaker's flub, error

G

gadol: huge, large; great one

"Gai avek!": Go away, get out of here.

"Gait es nit!": It doesn't work!

"Gai feifen afenyam": go whistle in the ocean

"Gait, gait!": Come now!

"Gai gezunterhait!": Go in good health; also, Go do your own thing, see if I care

"Gai in drerd arein!": Go to hell!

"Gai kakhen afenyam": Go shit in the ocean

"Gai mit dein kop in drerd: "Stick your head in the mud"

"Gai platz!": Go split your guts!

"Gai shlafen": Go to sleep.

"Gai shlog dayn kop en vant!": Go bang your head against the wall

"Gai shoyn, gai": Scram! also, Don't be silly!

"Gai strasheh di vantzen": You don't frighten me! (Lit, Go threaten the bed bugs)

"Gai tren zikh": Go fuck yourself

Galitsianer: Jewish native of Galicia

Galut: the Diaspora; exile

Gan Eden: the Garden of Eden

Ganif: crook, thief, scoundrel, rascal

25

Gants gut: very good

Gantseh K'nacker!: big shot

Gantseh Makher: big shot

Gantseh megilleh: big deal!

Gantseh mentsh: manly, an adult

Gaon: head of a Talmudic academy

Gatkes: long johns.

Geben shoykhad: to bribe

Gebentsht: blessed

Gebentsht mit kinder: blessed with children

Gebentshte boykh: to bless the womb of the mother with a wonderful child or children,

Gebrenteh tsores: utter misery

Gebrokhener english: fractured English

Gedainkst?: Remember?

Gedempte: slowly cooked.

Gedempte flaysh: mystery meat

Gedikht: thick, full, ample

Geferlekh: dangerous

Gefilte fish: dish made of chopped fish; fried or boiled.

Geharget zolstu veren!: Drop dead!

Gelaimter: clumsy person; one who drops whatever he touches

Gelibteh: beloved

Gelt: money. Khanuka gelt (chocolate coins) is given on the holiday

"Gelt gait tzu gelt": Money goes to money

"Gelt is nisht kayn dayge": Money is not a problem

Gembeh!: Big mouth!

Gemitlikh: slowly, unhurried, gently

Genaivisheh shtiklekh: tricky, sharp, crooked actions

Genevishe oygen: shifty eyes

"Genug iz genug.": Enough is enough!

Gesheft: business

Geshmak: tasty, delicious

Geshray: scream.

Geshtorben: dead

Geshtroft: accursed; punished

Geshvollen: swollen, puffed up

Gesundheit: (answer to a sneeze); health

Get: divorce

Getchke: statue

Gevaldikeh Zakh!: A terrible thing! (perhaps ironically)

Gevalt!: Terrible! Help! Ack! *See also* **Oy gevalt!**

Gevalt geshreeyeh: good grief!

Gezunde tzores: little troubles; trifling problems

"Gezunt vi a ferd": Strong as a horse

Gezunteh moid!: big healthy woman

Gezunterhait: good health

"Gib mir nit kayn aynorah!": Don't give me a canary!
    Don't give me the evil eye

"Gib zikh a traisel": Get a move on

Gib zikh a shukl: Hurry up! Shake a leg!

Gitte neshomah: good soul

Glatt kosher: strictly kosher.

Gleikhvertel: wisecrack, pun, saying

Glezel tai: glass of tea

Glezel varms: glass of warmth (soothing)

Glick: luck, bit of luck; "Glick in the office makes for glick in the home"

Glitsh: unexpected obstacle; slip up, bug; nosedive; glitch

"Gloib mir!": Believe me!

Glustiyah: enema

"G'nossen tsum emess!": The sneeze confirmed the truth!

G-d: (we all know who we're talking about, right?)

Goldeneh khasseneh: fiftieth wedding anniversary

Goldene medina: the golden country

Golem: a man-made humanoid; clumsy and sluggish; (Jewish legend: a protector and servant of Jews)

Gonif: *see* **Ganif**

Gopel: fork

Gornisht: nothing (more polite than bupkis)

Gornisht helfn: beyond help

Got in himmel!: G-d in heaven!

"Got tsu danken": Thank G-d

"Got zol ophiten!": G-d forbid!

Gote-Vorte: good info; concise Torah commentary

"Gotteniu!": Oh G-d!

Goy (pl. Goyim): non-Jewish person; Gentile (derogatory)

Goyeh: Gentile woman. *See also* **Shiksa**

Goyish(e): describing mannerisms of non-Jews

Goyishe kop: someone not smart or shrewd. (derogatory)

Goyisher: pertaining to non-Jew activity

Greps: Belch.

Grivenes: onions fried in chicken fat

Grob: coarse, profane, rude

Grober: uncouth or crude person

Grober finger: thumb

Grooten: to take after; to favor

Groyse: large

Groyse-makher: leader; self-appointed leader

Groyser tzuleyger: big shot

Groys-halter: show-off

Groysseh gedilleh!: Big deal!

Groysser gornisht: big good-for-nothing; fraud

Groysser potz!: Big penis! Big prick!

Groyser finger: middle finger

Grubber yung: rude young man

Guggle muggle: honeyed warm milk for sore throats

Gunsel: young goose; young tramp or follower

Guteneshoma: a good soul.

"Gut far him!": Serves him right!

Gut gezugt: well said

Gut Shabbos: Good Sabbath

Gut Yontif: Happy Holiday

G'vir: rich man

H

Haftorah: Talmud reading by the Bar Mitzvah boy

Haggadah: Passover storybook

Haymish: friendly; warm; informal; cozy; home-like; folksy

Haymish ponem: friendly face

Haiseh vanneh: hot bath

Haissen: to hate

"Haken a tshaynik": to knock a teakettle; boring, long-winded, annoying conversation

Hak flaysh: chopped meat

Hak mir nit in kop!: Stop bending my ear (Lit, Stop banging on

Halakha: Jewish law

Halevai (or alevei): I hope; It should come to be!

Halva: sesame candy

Hamoyn: common people

Handl: bargain; haggle

Handlen: to bargain; to do business

Hanoe hobn: to enjoy

Harte mogen: constipation

Hartsvaitik: heartache

Hashem, Ha-Shem: The Name; how to refer to G-d without naming God

Haskalah: Jewish equivalent of the 18th century Enlightenment in Europe

Hatikvah: Israeli national anthem

Havdala: a ceremony for the end of the Sabbath

Hekher: louder

hekhsher: kosher certification

Hefker: a mess

Heizel: whorehouse

Hekdish: slumhouse; a mess

Heldish: brave

Heldzel: stuffed neck flesh; like a neck-kishke

Hendl: chicken

"Hert zikh ein!": Listen here!

Heter (pl. heterim): halakhic ruling

Hetsken zikh: shake and dance with joy

Hikevater: stammerer

Hinten: rear, buttocks; in the rear

"Hit zikh!": Look out!

Hitsik: hothead

Hitskop: excitable person

"Hob derekh erets": Have respect

"Hob dir in arbel": I've got you by the elbow; Your words don't hurt me

"Hob nit kayn deyges": Don't worry

Hoben tsu zingen un tsu zogen: To sing and to talk; Have no end of trouble

Hoben groyse oygn: be greedy

Hoizer gaier: beggar

Hoizirer: peddler

Holishkes: stuffed cabbage

"Host du bie mir an avleh!": So I made a mistake. So what!

Huck: to bother incessantly; break; nag

Hulyen: hellraiser, hooligan

I

"Ikh bin ahntoisht": I am disappointed

"Ikh bin dikh nit mekaneh": I don't envy you

"Ikh darf es ahf kapores": I have no use for it!

"Ikh darf es vi a lokh in kop!": I need it like a hole in the head!

"Ikh hob dir lieb": I love you!

"Ikh eil zikh (nit)": I am (not) in a hurry

"Ikh feyf oyf dir!": I despise you!

"Ikh gai khaleshen bald avek": I'm about to faint (from exhaustion)

"Ikh hob dikh in bod!": To hell with you!

"Ikh hob dir!": Drop dead!

"Ikh hob dir in drerd": Go to hell

"Ikh hob es in drerd!": To hell with it

"Ikh hob im feint": I hate him

"Ikh hob im in bod!": To hell with him

"Ikh hob mir fer pakht": I have you in my pocket; I know your kind

"Ikh hob nikht kayn anung": I have no idea

"Ikh ken dir nisht farfeeren": I can't lead you astray

"Ikh loif": I'm running

"Ikh vais": I know

"Ikh vais nit": I don't know

34

"Ikh vel dir geben a khamalye": I'll give you such a smack

"Ikh vel dir geben kadokhes!": I'll give you nothing!

"Ikh yog zikh nit.": I'm not in a hurry

"Ikh zol azoy vissen fun tsores.": I should know as little about trouble (as I know about what you are asking me)

Iker: substance; people of substance

"In a noveneh:" for a change; once in a blue moon

"In di alteh guteh tseyten!": In the good old days!

"In di oygn:" to one's face

"In drerd mein gelt!": My money went down the drain!

In kaas oyf: angry with

In miten drinen: in the middle of; suddenly

Inyan: idea

Ipish: bad odor, stink

"Ir gefelt mir zayer.": You please me a great deal

"Iz brent mir ahfen hartz.": I have heartburn

K

Kaas: anger

Kabaret forshtelung: floorshow

Kabtzen, kaptsen: pauper

Kaddish: prayer of mourning; final prayer in synagogue

Kaddishel: baby son; endearing term for a male

Kadokhes: fever

Kadokhes mit koshereh fodem!: Absolutely nothing!

Kaftan: long coat of Orthodox Jews

Kahal: congregation

Kakameyme: nutty, rude. *See* **cockamamie**

Kakapitshi: conglomeration

Kalamutneh: dreary, gloomy, troubled

Kalleh: bride

Kalleh moid: nubile girl

Kallehniu: little bride

Kalta neshomeh: a cold soul

Kalekeh: new bride

Kalyeh: bad, wrong, spoiled

Kam derlebt: barely achieved

Kam mit tsores!: Barely made it!

Kam vos er krikht: just able to creep; slowpoke

Kam vos er lebt: He's barely alive

Kamtsoness: to be miserly

Kaneh: enema

Kapel or **Kippot:** skullcap for Jewish men at synagogue, or all the time. *See also* **Yarmulke**

Kaporeh: atonement; forgiveness; good for nothing

Kappora: catastrophe

Karabeynik: country peddler

Karger: miser, tightwad; dummy

Kaseer: enema

Kasheh: groats, buckwheat, porridge; mix-up, confusion

Kasheh varnishkes: cooked groats and bowtie noodles

Kashress: kosher; Jewish religious dietary law

Kashrus: kosher observance

Kasnik: angry person; hot head

Kasokeh: cross-eyed

Katchka: duck (bird)

Katshkedik: ducky; swell, pleasant

Katzisher kop: forgetful

Kaynahorah: the evil eye. Said aloud to ward off the evil eye

Kayn briere iz oikh a breire: Not to have any choice is also a choice

Kazatskeh: lively Russian dance

Kemfer: fighter; activist

Ken zein: maybe, could be

"Kenen oyf di finger": Have facts at one's fingertips

Kepi: small head

Ketzele: Kitten

Kibbitz: joke, talk, offer advice (uninvited)

Kibbitzer: meddlesome spectator

kibbutz: community co-op in Israel

Kiddish: blessing over wine on Sabbath eve or Festivals

Kike: derogatory term for a Jew.

Kikhel: biscuit.

Kimpet-tzettel: childbirth amulet or charm

Kimpetoren: woman in labor or immediately after

Kind un kait: young and old

Kinder: Children.

Kinderlekh: affectionate term for children

Kine-ahora: phrase to ward off the evil eye, or to declare that one's praises are genuine

Kippa: skullcap worn by observant Jewish males. *See* **Yarmulke**

"Kish mir en tokhes!": Kiss my butt!

Kishef makher: miracle worker

Kishka: guts, intestines, belly; sausage stuffed with a mixture of flour, onions, salt, pepper and fat to keep it together, boiled, roasted and sliced

Kitsel: tickle

Kh: *See* **Kh** category

Kleyne: small

Kleyner gornisht: little prig

"Klemt beim hartz": clutches at my heartstrings

Klaperkeh: talkative woman

Klipeh: gabby woman, shrew; female demon

Klog: plague

Klogmuter: chronic complainer

"Klog iz mir!": Woe is me!

Kloolye: a curse

Klop: bang; hard punch or wallop

Klotz kasheh: Foolish question; fruitless question

Kloymersht: as if; not really, pretended

Klutz: awkward or clumsy person; bungler; block of wood. *See* **Schlemiel**

Knacker: big shot; large diamond

Knackerke: female loudmouth

Knaidel (pl., **k'naidlekh**): dumplings of matzoh meal, cooked in soup

Knippel: button, knot; hymen, virginity

Knish: vagina; baked dumplings filled with potato, meat, liver or barley

Kokhalain: summer boarding house with cooking privileges

Kokhedik: petulant, excitable

Kokhleffel/Kukhleffel: gadabout, busybody

Kolboynik: impish know-it-all

Kol Nidre: Yom Kippur prayer

Kol tuv: all the best

Kop: head

"Kop oif di plaitses!": common sense!

Komisch: funny

Kopvaitik: headache

Kosher: Jewish dietary laws of "cleanliness"; legitimacy of a social or financial situation. *See also* treyf

Kosher glatt: very Kosher

Koved: respect, honor, reverence

Koyakh: energy

Krank: sick; annoying

Krank-heit: sickness

Krassavitseh: beauty, beautiful woman

Krekhts: groan, moan

Krekhtser: blues singer, moaner

Kreftik: hearty (food)

Kreplakh: dough like ravioli filled with chopped meat, eaten in soup; nothing, valueless

Kroivim: relatives

Krolik: rabbit

"Kuck im on!": Shit on him! The hell with him!

"Kuck zikh oys!": Go take a shit for yourself!

Kugel: noodle or potato pudding

"Kukn durkh di finger oyf": Shut one's eyes to, or wink at

"Kum ikh nisht heint, kum ikh morgen": If I don't come today, I'll come tomorrow (maybe)

Kumen tsu gast: to visit

Kuntzen: tricks

Kunts: accomplishment

Kunyehlemel/Kuni leml: naive, awkward person; nincompoop; nerd

Kuppe drek: piece of shit

Kurveh: whore, prostitute

"Kush in tokhes arein!": Kiss my ass!

Kushinyerkeh: cheapskate; penny-pinching

K'vatsh: spineless person; whiner; weakling

Kvell: feel great pleasure and pride

Kvetsh: complainer; to squeeze; gripe; whine; aggravating complaint

K'vitsh: shriek, scream

Kh

Khag Sameakh: happy festival

Khai: life

Khaider: religious school

Khaim Yonkel: any person at all

Khaimyankel kooternooz: the perennial cuckold

Khalaria: evil woman, shrew

Khalesh: faint

Khalishes: ugly

Khallah: Ceremonial "egg" bread, long or round

Khallish: to want something

Khaloshes: nausea, faintness, unconsciousness

Khametz: any bread with leaven in it

Khamoole: donkey, jackass, numbskull

"Khamoyer du ayner!": You blockhead! You dope!

Khanukah: the "Festival of Lights" is celebrated by lighting an additional candle each day for eight days.

"Khap a gang!": Beat it!

"Khap ein a meesa meshina!": May you suffer an ugly fate!

"Khap nit!": Take it easy! Not so fast!

Khaptsem: Catch him!

Khasid Khasidim: members of an orthodox religious sect.

Khassidus: teachings of the khassidim

Khassene: wedding

Khassene makhen: plan and do a wedding

"Khas v'kholileh!": G-d forbid!

Khaver: friend (male)

Khaverta: friend (female)

Khavarim: friends

Khaye: animal

Khayim Yankel: a hick, or just someone

Khayshik: enthusiasm.

Khazen: cantor, prayer leader

Khazenteh: Wife of khazen

Khazer: pig; voracious eater; jerk; dirt bag

Khazeray/khozzerai: junk; awful food; trash; pig's swill; unpalatable, rotten

Khazershtal: pigpen; slovenly room or house

Kheder: Hebrew school

Khei kuck: nothing, worthless, unimportant, dung

Khelm: a fairytale town of happy, foolish people

Khemye: Chemistry

Khesed: kindness

Khev 'r' mann: buddy

Khevra: group of friends

Khmalyeh!: Bang! Slam! Wallop!

Khokhem: wise man; wise guy

Khokhmeh: wisdom, witticism

Kholem: dream

Kholent: meat stew cooked overnight

Kholeryeh: cholera; a curse, plague

Khoshever mentsh: man of worth; respected person

Khosid: rabid fan

Khossen: bridegroom
Khossen-kalleh: bride and groom; engaged couple
Khoyzik makhen: make fun of, ridicule
Khrain: horseradish
Khropen: snore
"Khub Rakhmones": Have pity
Khug: activity group
Khupah: marriage canopy
Khutzpah: nerve, guts, daring, gall, audacity, effrontery
Khutzpenik: impudent fellow
Khvalye: ocean wave

L

Lakhen mit yash-tsherkes: forced laugh; laugh with anguish

Laidik-gaier: loafer

Lakeh: funnel

Lamden: scholar, learned man

Lamed Vovnik: Hebrew number "36." By traditional, each generation produces 36 wise and righteous persons who can be called "lamed vovnik."

"Lang leben zolt ir!": Long may you live!

Langeh loksch: very tall thin person

Lantslayt: plural of **lantsman**

Lantsman: countryman, neighbor, fellow townsman from the "old country"

Lapeh: big hand

Latke: Potato pancake, favorite for Khanukah

Layseh mogen: diarrhea

Lebedikeh Velt: lively world

Lebediker: lively person

"Leben ahf dein kop!": Well said! Well done!

"Lebst a khazerishen tog!": Living high off the hog!

Leck, shmeck: lick, smell; superficial once-over

"Lekhayim/L'khei-im/l'khayim!": To life! (traditional Jewish toast); To your health, Skol

L'hitraot: good-bye; see you later

Leffel: spoon

Leibtzudekel: sleeveless shirt with fringes, worn by orthodox Jews

Leiden: to suffer

Lemekhel: meek or quiet person

Lemeshkeh: bungler

Leshem shomaim: idealistically

Leveiyeh: funeral.

Lezem gayne: let them be

l'havdil: the difference; contrasting a great thing to one far less significant

"Lig in drerd!": Drop dead!

Ligner: liar

Litvak: Lithuanian Jew, often skeptical of Hasidic "magic"

Lobbus: little monster

Lokh: hole

Lokh in kop: hole in the head

Loksch: an Italian gentleman

Lokshen: noodles

Lokshen strop: a "cat-o-nine tails" whip

Lominer gaylen: golem created by the Lominer rebbe; clumsy fool

Lox: smoked salmon.

"Loz mikh tzu ru!": Leave me alone!

L'Shalom: to peace; to wholeness

L'Shem: G-d. *See* **Hashem**

Lubavitch: religious sect of Orthodox Jews

Luftmentsh: person who has no business, trade, calling, nor income; dreamer

Luzzem: leave him be; let her or him alone

M

Maggid (pl. maggidim): itinerant teacher; preacher

Makhareikeh: gimmick; contraption

Makher: big shot, important person, organizer

Makhetunim: relatives by marriage.

Makhshaifeh: witch

Maidel: Unmarried girl, teenager

Maideleh: Little girl

Maisse: story

Maisse mit a deitch: A story with a twist

Makhatanim: in-laws

Makeh: plague, wound, boil, curse

"Makh shnel!": Hurry up.

"Makhen a gevalt": make a scene, to scream and shout for help.

Makher: ambitious person; a schemer; *See also* "groyse makher."

Makheteyneste: in laws My makatenista are coming.(male= mkhutn)

Mameloshn: mother tongue, native language. Yiddish!

Mameleh: Mother dear

Mamoshes: people of substance

Mamzer: bastard child; untrustworthy

Mamzerook: naughty little boy

Mashgiakh: kashrut inspector for restaurants and hotels

Mashiakh, Moshiakh: the Messiah, defined by Jewish tradition

Mashugga: crazy. *See* meshuggeneh.

Matkes: underpants

Matzo: unleavened bread.

Matzo-brie: omelet of matzo mixed with egg omelette.

Maven: expert. *See* **Meyven**.

Maynster: mechanic, repairman

Mayster: master craftsman, champion

Mazel: luck.

Mazel tov: good luck; congratulations; or, sarcastically, "it's about time"

Meesa masheena: a horrible death

Meh: Who cares! (expression of indifference, belittling)

"Me ken brekhen!": You can vomit from this!

"Me ken lecken di finger!": It's delicious!

Mekheyeh: great pleasure

Mekhuten: in-law

Mekhutonim: in-laws

Mekhutainista: mother-in-law

"Me krekhts, me geht veyter": I complain and I keep going

Megillah: long boring story or discourse; the whole kit and kaboodle.

"Mein bobbeh's ta'am": Bad taste! grandma's style!

"Mein kheies gait oys!": I'm dying for it!

Mekhaye: delicious; a pleasure; orgasmic, wonderful!

Mekhuleh: bankrupt; wasted; ruined

Mekler: go-between

Melakha: work; labor specifically prohibited on Shabbat

Melamed: a teacher, especially of Hebrew language

"Me lost nit leben!": They don't let you live!

Menner vash tsimmer: men's room; restroom

Menorah: eight-branched candelabrum lit at Khanukah

Mentsh: person of character; honorable, decent human being (can be a man, woman or child)

Menuvel: person who get nothing right, and is always in the way

"Me redt zikh oys dos hartz!": Talk your heart out!

Meshpokha: extended family

Meshugah: crazy; senseless

Meshuggener: insane, crazy person

Meshugeneh: crazy, insane female

Meshugoyim: crazy people

Messer: knife

Metsiah: a find; a bargain price

Meyven: one who understands; expert; a know-it-all; enthusiast; connoisseur

Mezinka: special dance for parents whose last child is getting married

"Me zogt": They say; it is said

Mezumen: cash

Mezuzah: a small, oblong container set to the right of a Jew's front door-jamb, containing a tiny scroll of the Shema

Midrash: commentary; interpretation

Mies: ugly

Mieskayt: ugly person or thing; unattractive woman

Mikvah: bath for the ritual purity of Orthodox Jewish women just prior to marriage, as well as after each monthly cycle.

Milkhig: dairy foods

Minkha: daily religious service performed in late afternoon

Minhag: a custom

"Min tor nit": You mustn't

Minyan: quorum of ten adult Jews to hold a public worship service; in Orthodox Judaism only adult males are counted

Mirtsishem: G-d willing

Mishegas: mad idea, inappropriate, bizarre, crazy actions; insanity

Mishmash: hodge-podge

Mishpokhe: family; extended family; ancestors

Mitendrinen: right in the middle

Mitn derinnen: all of a sudden, suddenly

Mitn grobn finger: quibbling

Mitvokh: fortnight

Mitzvah (pl. mitzvot): commandment; good deed; good idea

Mizinik: youngest child in an immediate family

Mockers: put bad luck on something.

Mogen Dovid: Star of David

Mohel: religious circumcizer

Moisheh kapoyer: person who does everything backwards; not knowing what one wants

Moshe: Moses

Mosser: squealer

Mossik: mischief maker, prankster, naughty little boy, imp

Moyel/mohel: person or rabbi who performs bris (circumcisions on male babies)

Mutek: brave

Mutshe: to get on someone's nerves

Mutshen zikh: to sweat out a job

Muttelmessig: meddlesome person

N

Na!: Here! Take it.

"Nakh a mool": And so on.

Nakhes: joy; pride in one's children; doing good. *See* **Kvell**

"Nakht falt tsu.": Night is falling; twilight

Nadan: dowry

Nafkeh: prostitute; whore

Nafkeh bay-is: whorehouse

Naidlekhekh: rare thing

"Nar ainer!": You fool, you!

Narish: foolish

Narishkayt: silliness, foolishness; trivia

Narr: a fool

Narvez: nervous

Nebakh: It's a pity.

Nebbish: A nobody, simpleton; insignificant, pitiful person, awkward person, a loser, little nerd

Nebekhel: Nothing, a pitiful person; or playing role of being one

"Nekhtiker tog!": He's/it's gone! Forget it! Nonsense!

Nekhuma: consolation

Nekhvenin: to masturbate

"Nem zikh a vaneh!": Go take a bath! Jump in the lake!

Neshomeh: soul, spirit

Neshomeleh: sweetheart, sweet soul

"Nifter-shmifter, a leben makht er?": What difference does it make as long as he makes a living?

"Nisht geshtoygen/getoygen, nisht gefloygen": neither here nor there; it doesn't matter, it doesn't fit

Nishkosheh: not so bad, satisfactory

"Nisht araynton keyn finger in kalt vaser": loaf, not do a thing, be completely inactive

"Nisht fur dikh gedakht!": It shouldn't happen! G-d forbid!

Nishtgedeiget: don't worry; doesn't worry

Nisht geferlekh: not so bad, not dangerous

"Nishtkefelekht": No big deal!

"Nisht gefonfit!": Don't hedge. Don't fool around.

"Nisht getrofen!": So I guessed wrong!

Nisht gut: not good, lousy

Nisht naitik: not necessary

Nishtgutnick: no-good person

Nishtikeit: nobody; nothing, less than nothing.

"Nishtu gedakht!": It shouldn't happen! G-d forbid!

Nit kain farshloffener: A lively person

"Nit ahin, nit aher": Neither here nor there

"Nit gidakht!": It shouldn't happen!

"Nit gidakht gevorn.": It shouldn't come to pass

Nit kosher: impure food; anything not good

54

"Nit heint, nit morgen!": Not today, not tomorrow!

Nito farvos!: You're welcome!

Nitsn: to use

No-goodnik: bad guy

Nokh a mool: one more time

Nokh nisht: not yet

Nokhshlepper: hanger-on, unwanted follower

Nor Got vaist: only G-d knows

Nosh: (noun) snack; food not at dinnertime

Nosh: (verb) to snack; nibble; plagiarism

Nosher: nibbler

Nosherie: snack food

Nu?: So? Well? What's up? Hello?

Nu, dahf men huben kinder?: Does one have children? (When a child does something bad)

Nudzh: (verb) to nudge; remind; pester, bother, whine, badger

Nudzh: (noun) a pest; whiner

Nu, shoyn!: Move, already! Hurry up! Let's go!

Nudnik: pest, nagger, nuisance, a bore, annoying person

N'vayle: Shroud; inept person

O

Ober yetzt?/ober itzt?: So now?

Obtshepen: get rid of

"Okh un vai!": Alas; woe be to it!

Oder a klop/oder a fortz: either a wallop or a fart; either too much or not enough

Oder gor oder gornisht: all or nothing

Ohmain: amen

Oi!: *See* **Oy!**

Okurat!: That's right! Absolutely! Yah, sure!

Okuratner mentsh: orderly person

Olreitnik/alrightnik: solid middle-class

On langeh hakdomes!: Cut it short!

Ongeblozzen: conceited; peevish, pouting

Ongeblozzener: stuffed shirt

Ongematert: tired out

Ongepatshket: overdressed, mismatched, excessively adorned; too much; sloppy

Ongeshtopt/ongeshtopt mit gelt: very wealthy

Ongetrunken: drunk

Ongetshepter: useless hanger-on

Ongevarfen: cluttered, disordered

Onshikenish: hanger-on, pest

Onzaltsen: bribe; soft-soap; sweet-talk

Opgeflickt!: Done in! Suckered!

Opgehitener: pious person

Opgekrokhen: shoddy

Opgekrokheneh schoireh: shoddy merchandise

Opgelozener: sloppy dresser

Opgenart: cheated, fooled

Opnarer: trickster, shady operator

Opnarerei: deception

Orehman: poor man

Oremkeit: poverty

Ot azaih: that's how, just like that

"Ot kimm ikh": Here I come!

Ot gaist du: There you go again

Over Sholom: passed away

Oy

Oy!: "Oh!"; exclamation of surprise; disgust, pain; astonishment

Oy, a shkandal!: Oh, what a scandal!

Oybershter in himmel: G-d in heaven

Oy, gevald/gevalt: anguished cry; fear, shock or amazement

"Oy mi nisht gut gevorn": "Oh my, I'm growing weary."

Oyf tsalookhes: for spite

Oyfen himmel a yarid!: much ado about nothing!

Oyfgekumener: upstart

Oyfn oyg: Roughly, approximately

Oyg: eye

Oyg oyf oyg: face-to-face; privately

Oykh a bashefenish: A big shot, are you?

"Oykh mir a leben!": This you call a living?

Oysdruk: expression

Oysergeveynlekh: unusual

Oysgedart: skinny, emaciated

Oysgehorevet: exhausted

Oysgematert: tired out, worn out

Oysgemutshet: worked to death, tired out

Oysgeposhet: well-padded; fat

Oysgeputst: overdressed, overdone, overdecorated

Oysgeshprait: spread out

Oysgeshtrobelt!: overdressed woman

Oysgeshtrozelt: decorated, adorned

Oysgevapt: flat, flattened

Oys shiddekh: The marriage is off!

Oys-shteler: braggart

Oysvarf/oysvurf: dork; outcast, bad person

Oysznoygn fun finger: concoct a story

Oyver botel: absent-minded: getting senile

Oy-yoy-yoy: cry of of sorrow and lament

P

Paigeren: animal dying

"Paigeren zol er!": He should drop dead!

Pamelekh: slow, slowly

Parekh: low-life, bad man

Parnosseh: livelihood

Parsha (pl. **parshot**): weekly Torah reading

Parshiveh: mean, cheap

Parshoin: he-man

Partatshnek: inferior workmanship

Parev/parveh: foods that contain no meat or dairy products.

Paskidnye: rotten, terrible

Paskudnik: ugly, revolting, evil person; nasty fellow

Past nit: It isn't proper

Patsh: slap, spank, smack on the cheek (done gently to a child)

Patsh zikh in tukhis und schrei "hooray": Slap your backside and yell "hooray"

Patshkie around: waste time; fool around

Patteren tseit: lounge around; waste time

Payess or **payot:** long side-curls worn by ultra-Orthodox Jewish men

Pesakh: Passover.

Petseleh: little penis

Pfui!: show of disbelief, contempt

Pilpul: hair-splitting debate

Pinkt kahpoyer: upside down; just the opposite

Pipek: *See* **Pupik**

Pishekhtz: urine

Pish: to urinate

Pisher: male infant, bed-wetter; inexperienced person

Pisk: big mouth; mouth

Pisk-Malokheh: big talker-little doer!

Piste kayleh: a shallow person

Pitseler: toddler, small child

Pitshetsh: chronic complainer

Pitsel: wee, tiny

Pitsvinik: little nothing

Plagen: work hard, suffer

Plagen zikh: suffer

Plaplen: chatter

Pletzel: a solid bagel with poppy seeds and onion

Plimenik: nephew

Plimenitse: niece

Plotz: to burst, to explode in aggravation. Split your guts!!

"Platsin zuls du": May you explode

Plukhet: heavy rain

Plyoot: bull-shitter; loudmouth

Plyotkenitzeh: a gossip

Polkeh: chicken drumstick

Ponem/punim: face

Poo, poo, poo: Simulated spitting thrice to avoid the evil eye

Pooter veren: Getting rid of

Pooter veren fon emitzer: get rid of someone

Poseyakh: rolling out dough

Poskim: a halakhic ruling

Potchka: fool around; be aimlessly busy

Potshki: Experiment, dabble, mess around, play around with

Potzevateh: dimwit, slow person

Praven: celebrate

Preplen: mutter, mumble

Prezhinitse: scrambled eggs with milk added

Prietzteh: finicky girl; snooty; prima donna

Pripitchok: long narrow wood-burning stove

Prost: coarse, vulgar

Prostakhes: lower class people

Prostak: ignorant boor, vulgar man

Proster khamoole: Low-class shithead

Prosteh leit: common people; ignorant, lower class

Proster mentsh: vulgar man

P'shat: simple, obvious meaning

Ptsha: cow's feet in jelly

Pulke: upper thigh

Punim: face

Pupik: belly button, navel, gizzard

Pupiklekh: dish of chicken gizzards

Pushkeh: little box for coins

Pustunpasnik: loafer, idler

putz: penis; idiot, fool, patsy, jerk

Pyesseh: play, drama

R

Rakhmones: pity, compassion

Rebbe: rabbi.

rebbitzen: rabbi's wife; pompous woman

Rakhmones: Compassions, mercy, pity

Rav: rabbi, local religious leader

Rebbe fon Stutz: to explain the unexplainable.

Rebiniu: term of endearment for a rabbi

Reden on a moss: to chatter without end

Redn tzu der vant: talk and receive no answer

Redlshtul: wheelchair

"Redt zikh ayn a kind in boikh": imagined pregnancy

"Redt zikh ayn a kreynk!": imaginary sickness

Refuah shelaymah: full and peaceful healing

Reikh: rich, wealthy

Reisen di hoit: skin someone alive

Reissen: to tear

Rekhielesnitseh: dowdy, gossipy woman

Retsikhe: murder

"Ribi-fish, gelt oyfen tish!": Don't ask for credit! Cash on the barrel-head!

"Riboynoy-shel-oylom!": God in heaven, Master of the Universe

Rikhtiker khaifetz: The real article!

Rirevdiker: A lively person

Rolleh: role in a play

Rooshisher: person from Ukraine, White Russia; the Crimea, or Russia. Not a Litvak (*which see*)

Roseh: mean, evil person

Rosh Hashana: Jewish New Year

Rossel flaysh: Yiddish refritos

"Ruakh in dein taten's taten arein!": Go to the devil!

"Ruf mikh k'nak-nissel!": I did wrong? So call me a nut!

Ruktish: portable table

Rutzer: young, inexperienced

S

S'art eikh?: What does it matter to you?

Saikhel/saykhel/seykhel: common sense; using your head; intelligence

Sandek: person who holds the infant during bris (*which see*)

Se brent nit!: Don't get excited!

Seder: meals at first and second night of Passover.

Sefer: book

Seftr Torah: scroll containing the five books of Moses.

Sephadi: Sephardic; a Jewish person from Spanish or Portuguese and southern French descent.

"Se shtinkt!": It stinks!

"Se zol dir grihmen in boykh!": You should get a stomach cramp!

Siddur: prayer book

Simantov: a good sign; to wish someone good luck, to offer congratulations

Simkha: joy; a joyous occasion; celebration

Sitzfleish: sitting flesh; patience that requires sitting

Skeyne (pl. **Skeynes**): Old woman

Skeynim: old men

Slikha: excuse me

Slimp: crooked, bad

Smetana/smetteneh: sour cream; cream

Sobaka killev: doggy dog

Sof kol sof: finally

Sonem: enemy; someone thwarting your success

Spiel: *See* **Shpiel**

Spritz: *See* **Shpritz**

S'teitsh!: Listen! How is that possible? How come?

"Strasheh mikh nit!": Don't threaten me!

"Strashen net de genz": Do not disturb the geese. You are blathering nonsense.

Sufganiah (pl. **sufganiot**): jelly doughnut

S'vet helfen azoy vie a toytn baynkes: It will help as much as applying cups to a dead person

Sh

Sha!: Please keep quiet. Shut up!

Shabbas: Sabbath (Friday sundown to Saturday darkness)

Shabbat Shalom: Have a peaceful Sabbath

Shabbes goy: Someone doing the dirty work for others

Shabbes klopper: neighbor to "klop" or bang on shutters of Jewish homes at the hour of sundown on Friday

Shadkhen: professional matchmaker, marriage broker

Shaigetz (pl. **Sh'gootzim**) non-Jewish boy; unruly, clever, rascal

"Shaigetz ainer!": Jewish boy who flouts Jewish law

Shaile: question

Shailo: a judgement; ruling

Shain: pretty

Shaineh: lovely, wholesomely attractive; good

Shaineh kepeleh: pretty head; good looking, good thoughts

Shaineh maidel: pretty girl

Shaineh punim: pretty or beautiful face

Shaineh raaineh keporah: beautiful, clean sacrifice; nothing to regret

Shainer gelekhter: hearty laugh

Shainkeit: beauty

"Shain vi der lavoone": As pretty as the moon

"Shain vi di zibben velten": Beautiful as the seven worlds

Shaitel: wig. Some Ashkenazic Orthodox married women cover their hair with a shaitel.

Sha'koyakh: congratulations.

Shalakh mohnes: gift exchanges on Purim, usually goodies

Shalom: peace, deep peace; (used as a greeting)

Shalom aleikhem: formal greeting, to which the formal reply is aleikhem shalom:

Shammes: caretaker of a synagogue; also, the 9th candle of the Hanukkah menorah, by which all the other candles are lit in turn. Also, detective.

Shandeh: shame, disgrace, scandal.

Shandhoiz: brothel, whorehouse

"Shat, shat! Hust!": Quiet! Don't get excited

Shatnes: proscription against wearing clothes that are mixed of wool and linen

Shav: chilled soup made of sorrell cold spinach soup, sorrel grass soup, sour leaves soup

Shavuah Tov: Have a good week

shekhitah: ritual animal slaughter

Shema: *See* **mezuzah**

Shemevdik: bashful, shy

shemozzle: quarrel, brawl

Shepen nakhes/shep nakhas: enjoy; draw pleasure, especially from children

Shiddakh (pl., **shidukhim**): match, arranged marriage, or betrothal

Shihi-pihi: mere nothings

Shikker: drunkard; drunk

Shiksa: non-Jewish (Gentile) girl or woman (derogatory; better would be "goya")

Shik-yingel: messenger

Shissel: pot, basin or bowl

Shitter: sparse, lean, meager

Shivah: seven; seven-day period of mourning.

Shkapeh: hag, a mare; worthless

Shkotz: mischievous Jewish boy

Shlatten shammes: neighborhood busybody, gossip; messenger

Shlekht: bad; really bad

Shlekht veib: shrew; bad wife

Shlemazl: an unusually unlucky person

Shlemiel: klutz, idiot; a misfit; dummy; a born loser, bungler, a dolt

Shlep: drag, carry or haul; to make a tedious journey; to go somewhere unwillingly

Shlepper: a sloppy, lazy person, sponger, hanger-on; dowdy, gossipy woman

Shlissel: key

Shlokh: a shoddy, cheaply made inferior article; curse, apoplexy; a wretch, a miserable untidy person

Shlogen: to beat up

"Shlog zikh kop in vant.": Bang your head against the wall

"Shlog zikh mit Got arum!": Go fight with God

Shlong: large penis; snake, serpent; a troublesome wife

Shlookhe: slut

Shlosser: mechanic

Schlub: clumsy, stupid, or unattractive person; jerk. *See also* **Zhlub**

Shluff: to sleep, nap

Shlump (verb): to idle or lounge around

Shlump (noun): careless dresser, untidy, slouching person

Shlumperdik: unkempt, sloppy

Schmaltz: melted chicken fat; excessive sentimentality; flattery, overly emotional and sentimental, corny, gushing

schmatta/shmate/schmutter (pl. **shmates**): a rag; rubbish, cheap or unfashionable clothes; also low-quality merchandise; anything worthless

Shmeer: To spread (as in to "shmeer" butter on bread); to bribe; the whole works

Shmeis: bang, wallop

Shmeckle: small penis

Schmegeggy: idiot, dickhead, petty person, an untalented person, buffoon

Shmeikhel: to butter up; swindle, con, fast-talk

Shmek tabik: nothing of value

Schmeikel: To swindle, con, fast-talk

Shmendrik: a foolish or contemptible person, jerk, a stupid person, weak and thin pipsqueak, nincompoop; an inept or indifferent person. master of all jerks

Schmo: a naive person, stupid; idiot

Shmontses: trifles, folly

schmooze: to converse informally, make small talk or chat; coax with charming behavior

schmuck: self-made fool, contemptible person, a jerk; penis

Shmulky!: a sad sack!

Shmutz: dirt, speck of dirt; dirty language

Schmitzig: thigamabob, doodad

Shmutzik: dirty, soiled

Shmutzy: unkempt or dirty.

Shnapps: whiskey. *See also* **bronfen**

Shnecken: small fruit and nut coffee rolls

Shneider: tailor; in gin rummy, to win game before opponent scores

Shnell: quick, quickly

Shnide: to do something underhanded.

Shnook: a patsy, a sucker, a sap, easy-going, gullible; a cute or mischievous person or child

Schnorrer: beggar, moocher, cheapskate; mean person

Schnozz: a nose, especially a large nose

Shnur: daughter-in-law

Shoah: the Holocaust

Shofar: A ram's horn blown in synagogues on the new year, and for festivals

Shokhet: ritual slaughter of animals and fowl for kosher meat; animal slaughterer

Shokklen: to shake

Shoymer: watchman

Shoymer mitzves: pious person

"Shoyn ainmol a' metsei-eh!": really a bargain

"Shoyn fargessen?": You have already forgotten?

"Shoyn genug!": That's enough!

Shpatzir: walking without a destination

Shpiel: to play; elaborate sales pitch or persuasion

Shpilkes: pins and needles; nervous energy, worries; restlessness, impatience.

Shpits: end, the heel of the bread

Shpitsfinger: toes

Shpitzik: sarcastic wit, caustic comment

Shpogel nei: brand-new

Shpritz: spray or squirt

Shreklekheh zakh: terrible thing

Shtarben: to die

Shtark, shtarker: strong, brave

Shtark gehert: (food) smelled bad

Shtark vi a ferd: strong as a horse

Shteig: to accumulate wealth; to grow in wisdom

Shteln zikh oyg oyf oyg mit: to confront

Shtetl: A small village in Eastern Europe, all or mainly Jewish; Jewish ghetto village

shtiebel: (pl. **shtiebelekh**) little house, little room; a place for communal Jewish prayer; prayer room

shtik: routine, sketch; an actor's bit; defining habit or distinguishing feature; also, stick

Shtik drek: Piece of shit; shit-head

Shtik goy: heretic; person ignorant of Jewish religious values

Shtik nakhes: grandchild, child, or relative who gives you pleasure; a great joy

Shtikel: small bit; a morsel

Shtiklekh: tricks; small pieces

Shtilinkerait: quietly

Shtimm zikh: shut up!

Shtoltz: pride; stubbornly proud, excessive self-esteem

Shtrafeeren: to threaten

Shtrudel: sweet cake made of paper-thin dough rolled up with various fillings

Shtuk: trouble; in trouble

Shtunk: stinker, nasty person, smelly person; scandalous mess

Shtum!: Keep quiet! (to noisy children, or sharing a secret)

Shtup: have sex, screw, sexual intercourse; tip, shove

"Shtup es in tokhes!": Shove it up your ass!

Shtuss: minor unnecessary annoyance

Shudden: big mess

Shul: synagogue; school

Shushkeh: whisper; an aside

Shutfim: associates

Shvakh: weak, pale

Shvakhkeit: weakness

Shvantz: tail; penis

schvartze: black, illegal business; black people

schwartz yor: black year; bad luck

schwartzen sof: a bad end

Shvegerin: sister-in-law

Shvengern: be pregnant

Shver: father-in-law; heavy, hard, difficult

"Shvertz azayan Yid": It's hard to be a Jew

Shviger: mother-in-law.

Shvindel: fraud, deception, swindle

Shvindeldik: dizzy, unsteady

Shvitz (pl. shvitsn): to sweat, be hot, perspire; Turkish
bath house

Shvitzer: braggart, showoff

Shvitz bod: steam bath

Shvoger: brother-in-law

Shyster: thief, unscrupulous person

T

Ta'am: taste, flavor; good taste

Ta'am gan eyden: a taste of the Garden of Eden, fabulous

Takhlis: practical purpose, result

Tahkeh: Really! Is that so? Certainly!

Tahkeh a metsieh: Really, a bargain!?

Taiglekh: small pieces of little cakes dipped in honey

Tallis: Rectangular prayer-shawl with fringes attached to the four corners

Tallis katan: jacket worn underneath an Orthodox male's outer garment

Talmud: Jewish law and tradition.

Talmud: complete treasury of Jewish law, interpreting the Torah into livable law

Talmud Torah: commandment to study the Law; local school for orphans and poor children; in the U.S., a Hebrew school for children

Talmid khakham: expert on the Talmud

Tamavate: feebleminded

Tamaveter: feebleminded person

Tandaytneh: inferior

Tanta: aunt

Tararam: big noise, big deal

Tashlikh: Jewish New Year ritual for casting off sins

Tateh, tatteh, tatteh, tatteleh, tatinka, tatteniu: father, papa, daddy, pop

Tateh-mameh: papa-mama: parents

Tateniu: Father dear; also, G-d

Tateniu-Foter: G-d, our Father

Tefilla: prayer

Tchalish: eager, desperate for

Tchatchke: knick-knack, little toy, plaything, ornament, trinket, bric-a-brac; or, sexy girl, overdressed woman, pretty young thing (also, tchotchkala)

Tchepen: pester someone; banter

Tchiddush: the point, conclusion; innovation

Tefillin: phylacteries

Teyer: costly, expensive

Tei-yerinkeh!: Sweetheart, dearest

Temp: dolt

Temper kop: dullard

Teshuvah: repentance

"Ti mir nit kayn toyves": Don't do me any favors

Tinef: poorly made, junk

T'noim: betrothal, engagement

Todah Rabah: thank you

Tokhes: *See* **Tukhes**

Togshul: day school

"Toig ahf kapores!": Good for nothing! It's worth nothing!

Tokhis oyfn tish: put up or shut up

Torah: five books of Moses.

traif: non-kosher, forbidden food, contrary to Jewish dietary laws

Traifener bain: Jew who does not abide by Jewish law

Traifeneh bikher: forbidden literature

Traifnyak: despicable person; one who eats non-kosher food

Trefn oyfn oyg: to make a guess

Trenen: to tear, rip

Trepsverter: step words; the perfect retort you thought up after it was too late

Trogedik: pregnant

"Trog gezunterhait!": Wear it in good health!

Trombenik: bum, no-good person, ne'er-do-well; a faker

Tukhes: tush, rear end, bottom, backside, buttocks, derriere, fanny, ass

"Tukhes ahfen tish!": Asses on the table! Put up or shut up! Let's conclude this!

Tukhes in droissen: bare behind

Tukhes-lecker/tokhis leker: brown-noser, apple-polisher, ass-kisser

"Tu mir a toiveh.": Do me a favor

"Tu mir nit kain toives.": Don't do me any favors

Tumul: Confusion, noise, uproar, commotion, disorder

Tumler: an entertainer or emcee, especially one who encourages audience interaction; shouter, agitator

Tush: bottom, buttocks, rear end

"Tut vai dos harts": heartbroken

Ts

Tsaddik: pious, righteous person

Tsalookhes: spite

Tsalookhesnik: spiteful person

"Tsatskeleh der mamehs!": Mother's favorite! Mother's pet!

Tsatskele: bimbo

Tsebrekh a fus!: break a leg!

Tsedrait: nutty, crazy, screwy; mad person

Tsedraiter kop: bungler

Tseereh: face

Tseeshvimmen: blurred

"Tsegait zikh in moyl": It melts in the mouth, delicious

Tsemishnikh: confusion

Tsemisht: confused, befuddled

Tsetummelt: bewildered, confused. *See also* **Tumel**

Tsevishen-shtotisheh telefonistkeh: long distance operator

Tshepen: to annoy, irk, bother

Tsibele: onion; fried onions

Tsigeloisen: compassionate, rather nice

Tsiklen zikh: cantor's ecstatic repetition of a musical phrase

Tsimmes: *See* **Tzimmes**

Tsitskeh: breast, teat, udder

Tsivildivit: crazy, wild, overwhelmed with too many choices

Tsnueh: chaste

Tsores: troubles, serious woes, suffering, misery

"Tsu undzer tsukunft tzuzamen": To our future together

Tsutsheppenish/tsutcheppenish: hanger-on, pest, nuisance; obsession

"Tsum glik, tsum shlimazel": For better, for worse

Tsumakhn an oyg: to fall asleep

Tsvilling: twins

Tzaddik: holy man, righteous man.

Tzadrait: scattered

Tzedakeh: righteousness, justice; charity, philanthropy, benevolence

Tzefleiguene: empty-headed women

Tziginner bobkes: goat droppings; jocular, valueless; black olives.

Tzimmes: a sweet stew of vegetables and fruit, sweet carrot compote; a big deal made out of a minor matter, a fuss, an involved and troubling business

Tziter: to tremble

Tziterdik: tremulous or trembling

Tzitzis: fringes attached to the four corners of the tallis

Tznius: modesty

Tzufil!: Too much! Too costly!

U

Um-be-rufen: unqualified, uncalled for; God forbid; (to ward off the evil eye)

Um-be-shrien: God forbid! It shouldn't happen!

Umgeduldik: petulant

Ummeglikh!: Impossible!

Umglick: misfortune; born loser; an unlucky one

Umshteller: braggart

Umzist: for nothing

Umzitztiger fresser: free loader, one who shows up only to eat

Ungashtupt: overdone

Ungepatched: all mixed up

Unger bluzen: bad mood, swollen with anger, about to burst into tears

Ungerissen beheiman: untamed animal, really stupid person

Universitet: university

Un langeh hakdomes!: Cut it short!

Unter fir oygn: privately

Unterkoifen: to bribe

Untershmeikhlen: to butter up

Untershte sheereh: the bottom line

Untervelt mentsh: racketeer

Untn: below

Utz: to goad, to needle

Utzing: needling, bothering

V

"Vahksin zuls du vi a tsibeleh, mitten kup in drerd":
May you grow like an onion, with your head in the ground!

"Vahksin zuls du, tsu gezunt, tsu leben, tsu langeh yor":

May you grow to health, to life, to long years. (said when someone sneezes)

Vai!: Woe, pain

"Vai is mir!": Woe is me!

"Vai vind iz meine yoren": Woe is me!

"Vais ikh vos": Stuff and nonsense! Says you!

Vaitik: ache

Valgeren zikh: wander around aimlessly

Valgerer: homeless wanderer

Vaneh: bath, bathtub

Vannit: where (are you) from

Vantz: bedbug; a nobody

Varenikehs: round-shaped noodle dough stuffed with meat, potato, and fried

Varfen an oyg: to look out for; to guard; to mind

Varnishkes: kasha and noodles

Vart!: Wait! Hold on!

Vash-tsimmer: bathroom, washroom

Vash-tsimmer far froyen: ladies' restroom

Vash-tsimmer far menner: men's restroom

"Vayt fun di oygn,vayt fun hartsn": Far from the eyes, far from the heart.

Vekhter: watchman

Veibernik: debauchee

Veibershe shtiklakh: female tricks

"Veis vi kalekh!": pale as a sheet!

Vek-zaiger: alarm clock

"Vemen barestu?": Whom are you screwing? Whom are you kidding?

"Vemen narstu?": Whom are you fooling?

Verdreht: mixed-up, distracted

Verklempt: choked with emotion, all choked up

"Vei is mir": woe is me.

"Ver derharget": Drop dead, Get killed

Vershtupt: pregnant, constipated

Vielen dank: many thanks

"Vi gait dos gesheft?": How's business?

"Vi gait es eikh?": How goes it with you? How are you? How are you doing?

"Vi gaits?": How goes it? How are things?

"Vi haistu?": What's your name?

"Vi ruft men...?": What is the name of...?

"Vi ruft men eikh?": What is your name?

"Viazoy?": How come?

"Vie khavele tsu der geht": Like Khavele on her way; all spruced up. A song about Khavele reports her as an innocent person killed on her way to work

Vifil?: How much?

Vigorish/vig: that portion of gambling winnings held by the bookie as payment for services

Vilder mentsh: wild one; wild person

Vilda Chaya: wild animal, unruly child

Vilder khaiah: wild animal, out-of-control child or adult

Vilstu: Do you want..

"Vo den?": What else?

Voglen: to wander around aimlessly

Voiler yung!: Roughneck!

Voncin: bedbug

Vooden: What do you expect? What else?

Vort: explanation; discourse; opinion

"Vos vet zein, vet zein!": What will be, will be!

"Vos zogt ir?": What are you saying?

"Vu tut dir vai?": Where does it hurt?

"Vus du vinsht mir, vinsh ikh dir.": What you wish me, I wish you

"Vuhin gaitsu?": Where are you going?

Vund: wound

Vursht: bologna

"Vus machs da?": What's happening? What's up?

Vyzoso: idiot; also, penis

W

"Wen der tati/fater gibt men tsu zun, lakhen baiden. Wen der zun gibt men tsu tati/fater, vainen baiden.": When the father gives to his son, both laugh. When the son gives to the father, both cry

"Wen ikh ess, kh'ob ikh alles in drerd".: When I am eating, everybody can go to hell!

Witz: joke

Worsht (pronounced vorsht): salami

Y

Yakhna: a gossip.

Yakhneh: coarse, loud-mouthed woman; a gossip; slattern

Yakhsen: man of distinguished lineage, highly connected person

Yahrtzeit: anniversary of death of a loved-one

yarmulke: round cloth skullcap worn by observant Jews during prayers; worn at all times by observant Orthodox Jews. Same as **Kippa** and **Kapel**

"Yashir koyekh": May your strength continue

Yatebedam: man who threatens; a blusterer

Yedies: news; cablegrams; announcements

Yefayfiyeh: beauty; woman of great beauty

Yekke: a German Jew

Yeke: jacket

Yenavelte: in the middle of nowhere

Yenems: someone else's; mooched cigarette

Yeneh velt: the world to come

Yenta: female gossip; talkative woman, scold, busybody; she-devil

Yente telebente: gossip full of news

Yentz: coarse word for sexual intercourse; to cheat or screw someone.

Yentzer: cheater; fornicator

Yentzen: to fornicate, to whore

Yeshiva: Jewish traditional higher school, talmudic academy, rabbinical college

Yeshiver bukher: yeshiva student

Yeshuvnik: farmer, rustic

Yikhes: prestige, family status, ancestry, nobility

Yid (pl. **Yidden**): a Jew. "Yid" has been used as a derogatory term, and should be avoided by non-Jews.

Yiddish: language of Ashkenazi Jews of Eastern Europe, as evolved from German, Hebrew, Polish, Russian

Yontef or Yom tov: any Jewish holiday on which work is forbidden

Yiddishe: Jewish.

Yiddisher kop: Jewish head. Smart person.

Yiddishkeit: Jewishness; all things relating to Jewish culture

"Yingeh tsatskeh!": A living doll!

Yiskor: Prayer in commemoration of the dead

Yom Kippur: Day of Atonement (the most holy of holy days of the Jewish calendar)

Yontefdik: Festive, holiday-ish; sharply dressed

Yortseit: Anniversary of the day of death of parents or relatives

Yoysher: justice, fairness, integrity

Yukel: buffoon

"Yung mit bainer!": A powerhouse! Strongly built person

"Yung un alt": Young and old

Yungatsh: street-urchin, scamp, young rogue

Yungermantshik: young, vigorous lad; newlywed

Yusoimeh: orphan

Yutz: a fool; something or someone stupid

Z

Zaft: juice

Zaftik: pleasingly plump, juicy; buxom, full-figured as a woman

Zaftikeh moid!: sexually attractive girl

Zayer gut: very good, OK

"Zayer shain gezogt!": Well said! Well put!

Zaydeh: grandfather, old man

"Zee est vee a feigele": She eats like a bird

"Zeh nor, zeh nor!": Look here, look here!

"Zei gezunt/zeit gezunt": Be well! Goodbye! Farewell! Go in good health; Bless you (after a sneeze); To your health! (as a toast)

"Zei mir frailikh!": Be happy!

"Zei mir gezunt!": Be well!

"Zei mir matriakh": Please make an effort

"Zei nit a nar!": Don't be a fool!

"Zei nit kain vyzoso!": Don't be a damn fool!

"Zeit azoy gut": Please; Be so good

"Zeit ir dokh ahfen ferd!": You're on the horse! You're all set!

"Zeit mir moykhel": Excuse me! Be so good as; Forgive me!

Zelig: blessed (referring to a dear departed)

Zeltenkeit: rare thing

Zetz: Shove, push, bang!, punch ; sexual experience

"Zie ga zink": Wishing someone good health.

"Zi farmakht nit dos moyl": She doesn't stop talking, She doesn't shut her mouth

"Zindik nit": Don't complain. Don't tempt the Gods

Zingen: to sing

Zion: Jerusalem

Ziseh neshomeh: sweet soul

Ziseh raidelekh: sweet talk

Ziskeit: sweetness, sweetheart; dear child

Zitsen ahf shpilkes: sitting on pins and needles; fidgeting

Zitsen shiveh: Sit in mourning for seven days

Zitsflaish: patience

"Zog a por verter": Say a few words!

"Zogen a ligen": Tell a lie

Zogerkeh: woman who leads prayers in the women's section in the synagogue

Zoineh: prostitute

Zokn: old man

"Zok nit kin vey": Don't worry about it

"Zol dikh khapen beim boykh.": You should get a stomach cramp!

"Zol dir klappen in kop!": It should bang in your head!

"Zol er tsebrekhen a fus!": He should break a leg!

"Zol es brennen!": The hell with it!

"Zol Got mir helfen!": May God help me!

"Zol Got op-hiten!": May God prevent!

"Zol ikh azoy vissen fun tsores!": I haven't got the faintest idea!

"Zol makekhs voxen offen tsung!": Pimples should grow on your tongue!

"Zol vaksen tzibbelis fun pupik!": Onions should grow from your bellybutton!

"Zol ze vaksen ze ve a tsibble mit de kopin dreid": You should grow like an onion with your head in the ground

"Zol zein!": Let it be! That's all!

"Zol zein azoy!": OK! Let it be so!

"Zol zein gezunt!": Be well!

"Zol zein mit glik!": Good luck!

"Zol zein shah!": Be quiet. Shut up!!

"Zol zein shtil!": Silence! Let's have some quiet!

"Zolst geshvollen veren vi a barg!": You should swell up like a mountain!

"Zolst helfen vi a toyten bankes": It helps like like cupping helps a dead person

"Zolst hobn tzen haizer, yeder hoiz zol hobn tzen tzimern, in yeder tzimer zoln zain tzen betn un zolst zij kaiklen fun ein bet in der tzweiter mit cadojes!": I wish you to have ten houses, each house with ten rooms, each room with ten beds and you should roll from one bed to the other with cholera.

"Zolst leben un zein gezunt!": You should live and be well!

"Zolst ligen in drerd!": Drop dead!

"Zolst nit vissen fun kain shlekhts.": You shouldn't know from evil

"Zolst es shtipin in tokhes!": Shove it up your rectum!

"Zolst zein vi a lomp-am tug sollst di hangen, in der nakht sollst di brennen": You should be like a lamp, you should hang during the day and burn during the night!

"Zolstu azoy laiben!": You should live so!

"Zorg zikh nit!": Don't worry!

"Zuninkeh!": Dear son! Darling son!

Zh

Zhaleven: to be sparing, miserly

Zhlub: ill-mannered person, clumsy jerk; slob, uncouth

Zhu met mir in kop: buzzing in one's head

Zhulik: faker